Lua Haw

By Marc Lawrence

October 2021

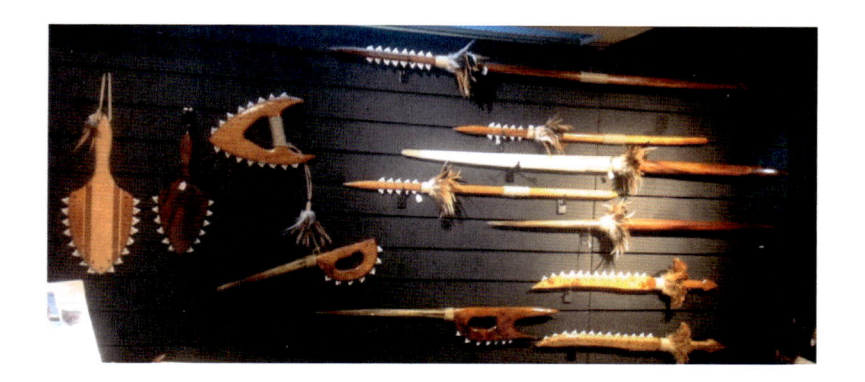

Table of Contents

Chapter-1 Historical Background   4

Chapter-2 The American Traders   13

Chapter-3 The Russian American Company 21

Chapter-4 Kapu Kuʻialua; Kuʻialua   31

Chapter-5 Introduction to Traditional Weapons 38

Chapter-6 Hand to Hand Methods   55

Chapter-7 Practice Drills with Weapons 58

Chapter-8 Making Your Own Training Aids 70

Chapter 9 Traditional Weapons Collections 77

References   88

Warnings

This book was written as a study of the use of Hawaiian Lua as combat fighting art from a historical and informative perspective.
You, the reader who purchased this book, or by reading this book, assume all personal and legal responsibility and liability for your own actions and safety, as well as the safety of others when and if you engage in training.

The author is not responsible for any stupid acts that someone does by not getting with a trainer/teacher or other stupid or unsafe acts. You do so at your own risk, "do not be dumb ass". Do not train with anybody who says "hey dude watch this" or any other stupid or questionable lack of judgement.

To quote Forest Gump "stupid is as stupid does"! Sharp blades and other weapons like Shark teeth and knives or swords cut really well, so remember to never use a blade on anything you do not wish to be cut! Enough said!

Chapter-1

Historical Background

  The history of **Kapu Kuʻialua**; **Kuʻialua** is one tied to Kingdom building and Hawaiian warfare. According to historians the Hawaiian Islands were discovered and settled Polynesians that arrived in Hawaii after navigating the ocean using only the stars to guide them. Traditional Polynesian navigators collected the information, watched the birds and debris in the water and marked positions of themselves mainly by the stars, using what today is called a star compass. A star compass was used to help memorize the rising and setting points of the brightest and most distinctive stars and planets to set direction. These star compasses were carved into the deck of the sail ships with each island identified that they learned was habitable.

  Navigators steer their waka (Outrigger Canoe) toward a star on the horizon. When that star rises too high in the sky or sets beneath the horizon, another is chosen, and so on through the night. Seven to 12 stars are enough for one night's navigation, and the moon and bright planets such as Kōpō (Venus) and Pareārau (Jupiter) are also useful.

As the islands were settled they were divided up into Chiefdoms. These Chiefdoms had warfare over control of areas and later islands due to needs for resources.

In 1778 The English explorer Captain James Cook lands at Waimea Bay on the island of Kauai, becoming the first European to make contact with the Hawaiian Islands. Cook names the archipelago the "Sandwich Islands" after the Earl of Sandwich.

1778 Cook's Voyage anchored at Kealakekua Bay on the island of Hawaii

In 1776, Cook sailed from England again as commander of the

HMS *Resolution* and *Discovery,* and in January 1778 he made his first visit to the Hawaiian Islands. He may have been the first European to ever visit the island group, which he named the Sandwich Islands in honor of one of his patrons, John Montague, the Earl of Sandwich.

Cook and his crew were welcomed by the Hawaiians, who were fascinated by the Europeans' ships and their use of iron. Cook provisioned his ships by trading the metal, and his sailors traded iron nails for sex. The ships then made a brief stop at Ni'ihau and headed north to look for the western end of a northwest passage from the North Atlantic to the Pacific. Almost one year later, Cook's two ships returned to the Hawaiian Islands and found a safe harbor in Hawaii's Kealakekua Bay.

It is suspected that the Hawaiians attached religious significance to the first stay of the Europeans on their islands. In Cook's second visit, there was no question of this phenomenon. Kealakekua Bay was considered the sacred harbor of Lono, the fertility god of the Hawaiians, and at the time of Cook's arrival the locals were engaged in a festival dedicated to Lono. Cook and his compatriots were welcomed as gods and for the next month exploited the Hawaiians' good will. After one of the crewmen died, exposing the Europeans as mere mortals, relations became strained.

On February 4, 1779, the British ships sailed from Kealakekua Bay, but rough seas damaged the foremast of the *Resolution,* and after only a week at sea the expedition was forced to return to Hawaii.

The Hawaiians greeted Cook and his men by hurling rocks; they then stole a small cutter vessel from the *Discovery*. Negotiations with King Kalaniopuu for the return of the cutter collapsed after a lesser Hawaiian chief was shot to death and a mob of Hawaiians descended on Cook's party.

The captain and his men fired on the Hawaiians, but they were soon overwhelmed, and only a few managed to escape to the safety of the *Resolution*. Captain Cook himself was killed by the mob. A few days later, the Englishmen retaliated by firing their cannons and muskets at the shore, killing some 30 Hawaiians.
The *Resolution* and *Discovery* eventually returned to England. This is the first European details of the Hawaiian fighting skills.

As the islands became increasingly populous, conflict erupted between the competing *ali'I* (rulers). The advent of the *kapu (forbidden)* system and the rise of the *ali'i* created a need for a specialized fighting force to protect the *ali'i* and act as a vanguard in actual combat.

The *na ali'i koa (Elite Warriors))* constituted a highly trained, disciplined and well-organized full-time unit of lesser *ali'i*, in contrast to the *na koa*, an army of commoners called into action during wartime. The commoners were give much less training.

Kamehameha, the *ali'i* who unified the islands under his own rule, entered training as a *na ali'i koa* in the 1840s when he was 7 or 8 years old according to historians.

This training usually fell to personal tutors and included a great deal of hand-to-hand combat known as **Kapu Kuʻialua**; this consisted of bone-breaking form of wrestling.

The training included well as the use of an assortment of deadly handheld weapons. These included the *pahoa*, a long, double-edged hardwood dagger, sometimes fitted with shark's teeth; the *niho 'oki*, a curved wooden knife with a single shark's-tooth blade; and the *ma'a*, a sling fashioned of braided fiber from the inner bark of the *hau* (coastal hibiscus) tree, a coconut husk or even human hair.

Other weapons used by the *na ali'i koa* included the *pohaku newa*, a war club comprising a carved stone head lashed to a wooden handle with a fiber cord, and the *ku'ia*, a quarter staff about 6 feet long and sharpened at both ends. Spears were also common. Shorter versions, like the javelin like *ihe*, were meant to be thrown, while longer spears, such as the *pololu*, were meant to be used like European pikes. The latter was very long and heavy, requiring a warrior of great strength and skill to effectively wield it. Another common weapon was the *ko'i pahoa*, or stone adze, employed much like the battle-axes used by the Vikings and other European warriors. *Na ali'i koa* later trained to use firearms. Petroglyphs at Kaloko-Honokohau National Historical Park on the Big Island include depictions of muskets alongside men. Historians believe the area likely served as a training ground for the *na ali'i koa*.

Kamehameha was the son of Keoua, a high-ranking *ali'i* on the Big Island. He was born sometime around 1736, a time of constant power struggles among the archipelago's *ali'i*. As Keoua died when Kamehameha was still a boy, he was raised in the court of his uncle, Kalani' opu'u. While there Kamehameha began training with his uncle's *na ali'i koa*. He learned the skills quickly and was reportedly an expert warrior by young adulthood.

On Kalani'opu'u's death in 1782, Kamehameha rose to prominence. Kalani'opu'u's son Kiwala'o inherited the kingdom and gave his cousin Kamehameha control of the Waipio Valley, to the north, as well as symbolic guardianship of the Hawaiian god of war, Kuka'ilimoku. The relationship between the cousins was strained at best, and soon after the funeral, when Kamehameha made a dedication to the gods instead of paying homage to Kiwala'o, the scene was set for conflict.

That same year Kiwala'o's half-brother Keoua Ku'ahu'ula, who had inherited no property after his father's death, went into a jealous rage, felling coconut trees in Kamehameha's district and killing some of his men. Adding insult to injury, Keoua offered their bodies as a sacrifice to Kiwala'o, who accepted the offering. Kamehameha had no choice but to defend his honor. Recognizing the omens, women and children from both sides fled to Pu'uhonua O Honaunau, a place of refuge on the west coast where they would be safe no matter the outcome.

The resulting Battle of Moku'ohai (a grove to the south of Kealakehua Bay) was fought on land and sea, with both *ali'i* fielding their *na ali'i koa* as shock troops in forward echelons. It was a fierce battle, and one of Kamehameha's chief supporters, Kame'eiamoku, was among the first seriously wounded when tripped up by a *pololu* and stabbed. Kiwala'o saw him fall and dashed in for the kill, but before he could deliver a fatal blow, a sling stone knocked him down. The injured Kame'eiamoku then slit Kiwala'o's throat with a shark-toothed *pahoa*. The king's abrupt death left the battlefield to Kamehameha and his warriors, and they took over the northern and western districts of the Big Island.
But Kamehameha set his sights far higher.

Though no firearms were reportedly used at the 1782 Battle of Moku'ohai, the Hawaiian *ali'i* were broadly aware of European weaponry as early as 1778. That year British explorer Captain James Cook and his contingent of sailors and marines aboard HMS *Resolution* anchored off the coast of Kauai, becoming the first Europeans to visit the remote islands. He collectively dubbed them the Sandwich Islands, after his patron John Montagu, 4th Earl of Sandwich (and, yes, reputed progenitor of *that* sandwich).

Kamehameha witnessed much of what transpired and was intrigued by the power of the European firearms. He understood that mastering such weapons would enable him not only to defeat his enemies but also to be a deterrent to outsiders seeking to conquer the islands. In 1789 the ambitious *ali'i* persuaded Scottish-born fur trader Captain William Douglas, who was wintering in the islands aboard the merchantman *Iphigenia*, to give him muskets, ammunition and a swivel gun, ostensibly to protect the Big Island from enemies supplied with weapons by Douglas' rivals. Kamehameha's desire for firearms only grew.

Chapter 2

The Americans

In 1790 American trader Simon Metcalfe, captain of the brig *Eleanora*, arrived off the Big Island and immediately overstayed his welcome by having Kamehameha's trusted counselor Kame'eiamoku flogged for some offense. Moving on to Maui, Metcalf and crew soon found themselves in a more serious skirmish with islanders and used their cannons and muskets to great effect against the attackers.

Meanwhile, *Eleanora*'s sister ship, *Fair American*, captained by Metcalfe's son Thomas, dropped anchor off the Big Island. Unaware of the family ties between the captains, but having sworn revenge against the next Western ship to visit, Kame'eia-moku directed his men to attack *Fair American*. They killed all aboard but wounded Seaman Isaac Davis, whom Kamehameha ordered into protective custody. In the wake of that incident, Kamehameha detained *Eleanora*'s boatswain, John Young, who had come ashore to ask after *Fair American*'s missing crew. Treated well, the two American sailors soon became trusted advisers and, later, *'ohana* (family) through marriage to the *ali'i*'s family members. They also instructed Kamehameha's warriors in the use, maintenance and repair of firearms, training that forever changed Hawaiian combat tactics.

By then the Sandwich Islands had become a popular stop-off on the Pacific trade route between the Americas and China. Subsequent British and

American traders, always eager to turn a profit, were more than willing to trade firearms and gunpowder with the Hawaiian *ali'i*.

Kamehameha proved even more resourceful, soon obtaining the formula to make his own gunpowder. Its ingredients—sulfur, potassium nitrate and charcoal—were plentiful in the islands, and with traders regularly bringing lead, the *ali'i* soon stored up all the ammunition he needed.

Though the Westerners traded freely with Kamehameha, they also provided firearms and ammunition to the other *ali'i*, some of whom openly opposed Kamehameha. It was the latter's leadership and ability to earn the trust and loyalty of his people, particularly the *na ali'i koa*, that made him successful. The addition of Western weaponry was icing on the cake.

Statue of Hawaiian Warrior with Musket

    After securing victory at Moku'ohai, Kamehameha began his quest to unify the islands. He first had to gain complete control of the Big Island. Between 1783 and '90 he led repeated assaults against Keoua's stronghold in the southern Kau district. But the latter's forces had allied themselves with the *ali'i* of Maui, bolstering their ability to resist, thus in 1790 Kamehameha resolved to first subdue Maui. To do so, he had to risk fighting on two fronts. If the gamble paid off, he would win big—if not, he stood to lose everything. Leading the charge on both fronts were Kamehameha's *na ali'i koa*.

With most of its best warriors deployed to Hawaii in support of Keoua, Maui was left lightly defended, and Kamehameha's men ravaged the island. But word that Keoua was raiding his territory back on the Big Island forced Kamehameha to turn back before he could consolidate his gains.

Later that year Kamehameha moved against Puna, in the southeastern Big Island, coming up against forces led by Keawema'uhili, an *ali'i* loyal to Keoua. Though both armies were equipped with firearms, the battle was mainly fought using traditional Polynesian weapons and tactics—at which Kamehameha's *na ali'i koa* excelled. Kamehameha led by example, moving among his warriors and reportedly shouting, *"I mua, e na poki'i, a inu 'i ka wai 'awa'awa!"* ("Forward, young brothers, and drink the bitter water!"). The sight of their leader dodging spears and grappling with the enemy motivated his warriors to rally—enough to carry the day.

On Oahu Kamehameha's forces pushed their opponents upward through the Nu'uanu Valley and, ultimately, over a 1,000-foot cliff.

    With Kamehameha engaged in Puna, Keoua sensed an opportunity and led an uprising. It was ultimately unsuccessful, and as Keoua retreated toward Kau, an eruption of Kilauea killed many of his men. It was a bad omen from Pele, the goddess of fire, and within months warriors allied with Kamehameha lured Keoua and his *na ali'i koa* into an ambush and slew them to a man. With his rivals on the Big Island subdued or dead, Kamehameha became the undisputed *ali'i nui*, or high chief, of Hawaii. Contesting his efforts to subdue the remaining islands, the respective *ali'i* of Kauai, Maui and Oahu

 joined forces against him in 1791. After amassing a great fleet of war canoes, they set sail for the northwestern coast of Hawaii, where they fought Kamehameha in the Battle of the Red Mouth Gun.

It was a unique fight, both for the scale of the naval battle and the numbers of muskets and cannons used. Until that engagement most fights at sea around Hawaii had been little more than clashes of canoes in which combatants threw or thrusted with spears. But on that day the opponents employed canoes fitted with small, swivel-mounted guns, whose fire inflicted significant casualties and destroyed many vessels. Kamehameha watched from the deck of *Fair American* as his well-trained warriors—under the watchful tutelage of Young and Davis—laid waste to the enemy fleet.

The Battle of the Red Mouth Gun

The long war had taken its toll on the *ali'i* and warriors of all islands, and over the next four years of relative peace the combatants licked their wounds and regained strength. During the respite Kamehameha continued training his forces, especially *the na ali'i koa*, and in 1795 he was ready to resume his quest to claim sole control of the islands.

By early 1795 Kamehameha had amassed upward of 1,000 war canoes and an army of more than 10,000 men to move against his enemies. His first objectives were Maui and Molokai, whose combined forces he defeated at the Battle of Kawela on the latter island. From there he moved against Oahu, where he confronted the warriors of that island and Kauai.

Fought that May, the Battle of Nu'uanu was the largest and bloodiest engagement of Kamehameha's quest to rule the islands. The armies met on the southeastern side of Oahu, near present-day Honolulu. On landing at Waialae and Waikiki, Kamehameha's forces fought a 6-mile running battle, pushing the defenders northward into the Nu'uanu Valley. Kamehameha failed to notice his enemy had carved gun emplacements into the high ground and had been drawing the attackers into a deadly trap.

Despite heavy cannon fire from the heights, however, Kamehameha's forces continued to press the enemy into retreat. Realizing he had to silence the enemy's guns, Kamehameha ordered two groups of *na ali'i koa* to scale the cliffs of Nu Uanu Pali and get behind the guns. The elite warriors did so, surprising the enemy gunners and seizing control of the ridge. With the cannons silenced, the fighting turned to bloody hand-to-hand combat.

Through a series of skirmishes Kamehameha's warriors eventually forced their enemy, whose strength had dwindled to 800 men, to the razor's edge of the pali for a last stand. Rather than be captured and face enslavement or ritual sacrifice, most defenders fought to the death, many literally being driven over the edge of the 1,000-foot cliff at their backs.

Though Kamehameha had yet to bring Kauai and Niihau under his dominion, Nu'uanu proved the deciding battle of the war. Finally, in 1810 Kaumuali'i, the last independent ruler of Kauai, relinquished control of that island and Niihau to Kamehameha, making the latter *ali'i nui* of all the Hawaiian Islands. His victory in the long fight for unification was due in large part to the skill, dedication and loyalty of his *na ali'i koa*.

Chapter 3 -The Russian American Company

Russians in Hawai`i

In 1741, the discovery of pelt mammals in the Alaskan wilderness by the Russian explorer Vitius established a lucrative trade circuit between Russian and Chinese merchants. In 1799, the Imperial Russian Government granted the Russian American Company (RAC) sole authority to trade in the American territories. The imperial government appointed RAC's manager, Alexander Baranov, governor of Russian America. By 1804, Baranov had established a permanent trading port at Sitka, Alaska, known at the time as "New Archangel." The company built fortified settlements in the North Pacific, giving it an advantage over roving British and American traders. Eventually Russians established a presence in Hawai'i as merchants from around the globe demanded fragrant Hawai'i sandalwood.

The first Russian contact with Hawai'i occurred in 1804 when the *Nadezhda* and the *Neva*, commanded by Lieutenant-Captain Ivan Fedorovich Krusenstern and Lieutenant Iurii Fedorovich Lisianskii, visited O'ahu and Kaua'i. At this time Kamehameha was still consolidating his rule. Following Kamehameha's victory over neighboring islands in 1806, he offered to supply Baranov with foodstuffs and supplies in exchange for otter pelts.

The following year, the *Nikolai,* a small vessel under Captain Pavel Slobodchikov, detoured to the Islands while en route from California to Sitka. Slobodchikov was treated well by Kamehameha who furnished a cargo of foodstuffs in exchange for furs.

In 1808, Baranov sent the *Neva* under Lieutenant L.A. Hagemeister to the Islands for a supply of salt. Historians to this day debate whether this voyage was meant as a colonizing voyage and part of a larger push for Russian representation in America or merely a supply run. Hagemeister left Hawai'i without taking any immediate aggressive steps, but as he sailed away, he wrote out plans for colonizing the Islands. He was particularly interested in Moloka'i, but Baranov took no action on Hagemeister's report. Baranov instead attempted to place two settlements on the West Coast of North America to obtain agricultural produce and establish new bases for hunting sea otters. An expedition to the Washington coast met with prompt failure, but a more successful try in 1812 established Fort Ross in California.

American and British traders now became embroiled in the War of 1812. Baranov saw the conflict as an opportunity for profit. Several American traders sold their ships to Baranov at reduced prices rather than face the possibility of having them captured or sunk; American captains often continued to sail the vessels under contract with the RAC. One of these ships, the *Bering,* sailed to Hawai'i in late 1814 for a load of provisions. After stopping on Kaua'i, Maui and O'ahu, the ship ran aground in Waimea Bay during a gale. Stranded on Kaua'i for more than two months, the shipwrecked men eventually received passage off the island in April 1815 on the *Albatross*. Kaua'i islanders under Chief Kaumuali'i retained the ship's cargo of furs and the castaways' personal possessions. Baranov dispatched Georg Anton Schaffer, a German physician, to recover the ship's goods; if successful, he was to also negotiate permanent trade relations with the Hawaiian Islands. To give the mission a peaceful appearance, Schaffer arrived in Hawai'i on the American ship *Isabella* and posed as a naturalist.

     Schaffer immediately ran into huge opposition from John Young, John Ebbet, and W.P. Hunt, Britains and Americans close to Kamehameha. However, he eventually won Kamehameha's trust through the successful medical treatment of the king and his wife, Ka'ahumanu. In return, Kamehameha awarded Schaffer some land in Honolulu. In early May 1816, Schaffer established a post for his activities in Honolulu, where he raised the Russian flag. Other RAC personnel soon arrived on the *Ilmen* and the *Kadiak* and helped build a blockhouse. Schaffer proceeded to Kaua'i to negotiate the return of the *Bering's* cargo, apparently with a letter of support from Kamehameha. When Kamehameha discovered the Russians were building a fort and had raised the Russian flag in Honolulu, he sent chiefs from Hawai'i to remove the Russians from O'ahu by force if necessary. RAC personnel judiciously chose to sail for Kaua'i instead of risking bloodshed. The partially built blockhouse was finished by Hawaiians under the direction of John Young and 60 mounted guns protected the fort.

     When Schaffer met Kaumuali'i on Kaua'i, the high chief agreed to return the cargo still in his possession and to pay restitution in sandalwood for any items that could no longer be accounted for. Kaumuali'i asked that Kaua'i- the only island not yet conquered by Kamehameha - be placed under Russian protection and he granted the Russians a sandalwood trading monopoly. Schaffer and Kaumuali'i signed a "secret treaty" July 1, 1816: Kaumuali'i was to provide 500 men for the conquest of O'ahu, Lana'i, Maui and Moloka'i; Schaffer was to provide brigs, weapons and ammunition in trade for a sandalwood monopoly. Schaffer was also to oversee the construction of new forts and trading posts. Russian American Company employees and more than 300 native Hawaiians, including Kaumuali'i's wives, built Fort Elisabeth under this pact. Kaua'i chiefs and chiefesses also granted land to Schaffer and other RAC employees in leeward Waimea, Makaweli and Hanapepe. Kaumuali'i granted Schaffer the entire district of Hanalei on the north (windward) shore where Schaffer began building two forts, Alexander and Barclay. Using furs as barter, Schaffer purchased two American ships for Kaumuali'i, the *Lydia* and *Avon*.

Rumors of hostile Russian warships reached Kamehameha by late 1816. When the Russian naval ship *Rurik* under the command of Lieutenant Otto von Kotzebue arrived in Hawai'i in December 1816 during its around-the-world voyage, it was met by 400 Kamehameha loyalists armed with muskets. Kotzebue quickly made it known that he had no intention of conquest and he eventually sailed from Hawai'i without ever visiting Schaffer on Kaua'i.

Observing Kotzebue's behavior, Kaumuali'i now concluded Schaffer did not have the support of the RAC and he ordered Schaffer and his employees to leave Kaua'i. Schaffer left on the *Panther* with most of the RAC employees leaving shortly after on the *Ilmen*. Others on the *Kadiak*, however, were stranded when their ship ran aground in Honolulu where between 60 and 100 RAC employees remained until the spring of 1818. By 1818, Leontii Hagemeister had replaced Alexander Baranov as chief manager of the Russian American Company. Hagemeister thought occupation of the Hawaiian Islands was worthwhile but criticized Schaffer for going beyond the bounds of his authority and initiating "plans that could not be realized by available local resources."

In October 1818, Vasilii Golovnin on the *Kamchatka* made a brief visit to Kaua'i where he observed an English flag flying over the fort. He attempted to obtain an interpreter to talk to Kaumuali'i, but finding none, he sailed from the harbor without ever leaving his ship.

The strained relations between the RAC and Hawaiian chiefs had a severe economic impact on Russian's North Pacific colonies. Schaffer's expenses in Hawai'i were high and the Russians had lost many of their sources for provisioning.

In 1819, the Russian American Company purchased the ship *Brutus* from American traders and sent it to Hawai'i under Karl Johan Schmidt to buy provisions and reestablish normal trade relations between the Hawaiian Islands and the RAC. Schmidt was also to reclaim RAC belongings left on Kaua'i, but Kaumuli'i believed he deserved further payment for provisions used by Schaffer and his party.

Meanwhile, Schaffer had gone to China and then Europe to promote Russian annexation of the Hawaiian Islands. He was aided by a Swede named Anders Ljungstedt and Peter Dobell, an Irishman who supported Russian colonization of the North Pacific. In 1819, Dobell met with Kamehameha II (Liholiho), who had succeeded his father, Kamehameha I.

Although the Islands were under English protection, Dobell believed securing them for Russia would be simple. He noted that Hawaiians had given up their traditional religion, referring to the recent ending of the kapu system, and were "looking for a new religion." He recommended the RAC send a commercial agent, two priests, ornaments for a church and decorations for Liholiho. Ultimately, however, the Russian Foreign Minister Count Nesselrode did not take action on any of Schaffer, Ljungstedt, or Dobell's recommendations. He opposed all plans for colonization for fear of disrupting relations with the British and rousing the Americans who had established an increasing presence in Hawai'i.

By the 1820s, Russian colonies could get most provisions more cheaply from Boston or New York than from the Hawaiian Islands, but the salt trade between the North Pacific and Hawai'i continued. In 1821, the *Thaddeus* - the same ship that carried the first Protestant missionaries to Hawai'i in 1820 - sailed from Hawai'i to Kamchatka with a load of salt and other supplies after Petr Ivanovich Rikord, governor of Kamchatka, wrote to Liholiho requesting salt be traded for furs. Adol'f Etolin made a similar trip in 1822 on the *Golovnin*.

Russian vessels arrived in Hawai'i sporadically for years to come, but two visits in 1824 marked the last significant Russian voyages to the Islands. In early 1824, Lieutenant Khromchenko sailed from Sitka to Honolulu on the *Rurik* to obtain provisions to remedy an extreme shortage of food in the northern colonies. When Kaumuali'i died suddenly in Honolulu, the Russians did not join the rest of the ships in the harbor in giving a salute. Seven months later, Otto von Kotzebue returned to Honolulu on the *Enterprise*. Kotzenbue witnessed the end of a rebellion on Kaua'i that broke out after Kaumuali'i's death. Forces loyal to the Kamehameha line put down the rebellion. Kotzebue sent a message of congratulations to the victors to demonstrate Russia's support of the Kamehameha monarchy but Russia's influence in Hawai'i had declined and her hopes of colonizing Hawai'i had clearly ended.

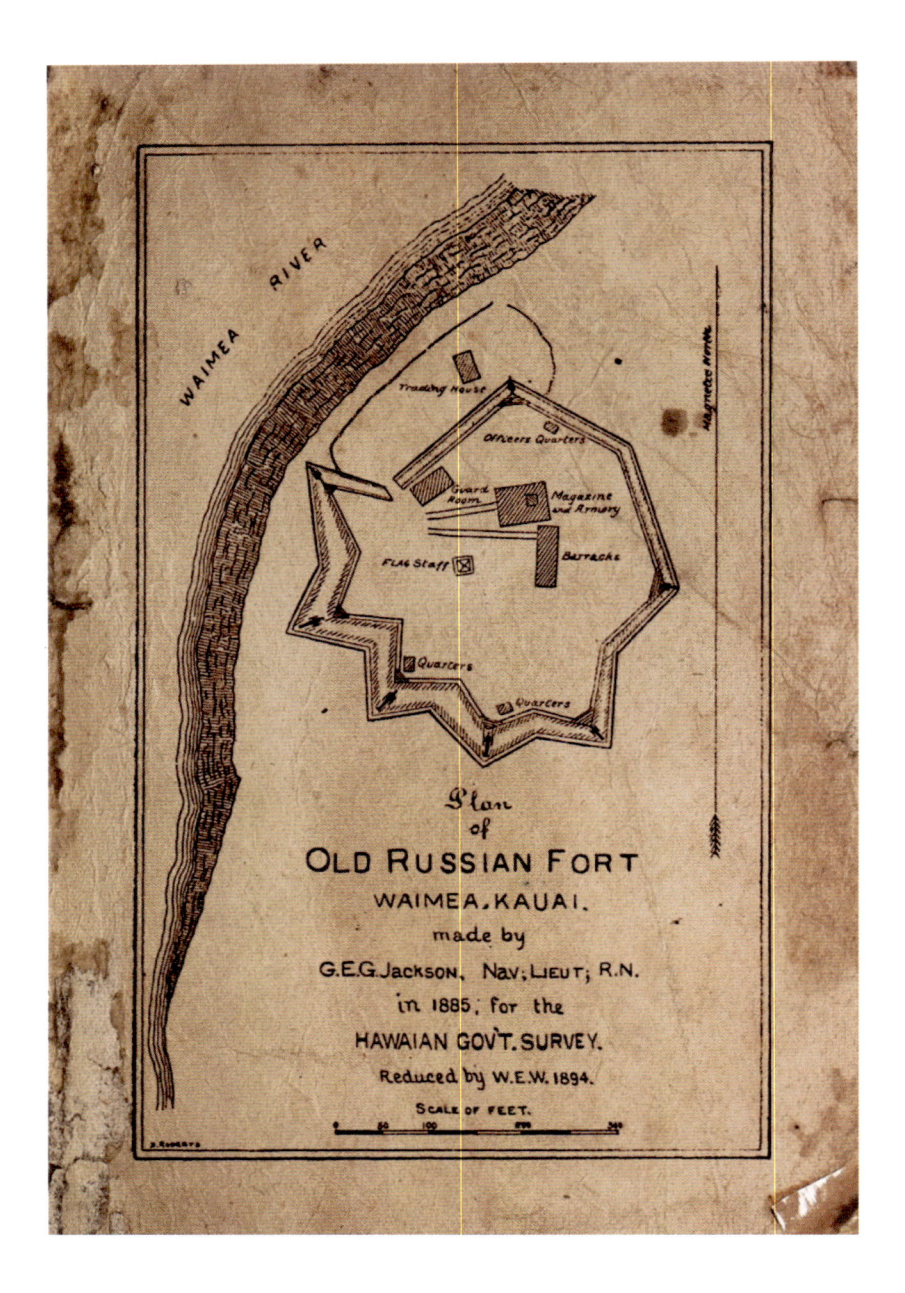

Fort Elizabeth

Illustration of the grounds of Fort Elizabeth

Fort Elizabeth as illustrated

Chapter 4 Kapu Kuʻialua; Kuʻialua

First what is Lua? Lua is the generic term for the traditional martial art of Hawaii. It comes from the term-**Kapu Kuʻialua; Kuʻialua. Where is it from? It is from Hawaii.** When we talk about Hawaii we are talking about the Kingdom of Hawaii. It was used by the Native Hawaiians.

This was shared with me- Huna Na Mea Huna, Keep secret what is sacred. But Teach, That Lua might not be lost. Charles Kenn told his five Haumana (students) that he graduated as Olohe (Lua masters)

How did I come to learning about Lua, I read an article about it in a magazine and how they were teaching Native Hawaiian about it. It was few years later that I met a "Kuma" teacher of the Lua named Michel Manu. She has taught some to my friends, my family and myself. She is the only female Kuma I know of. Her stories of training and how the men did not think she would not have the fortitude to complete the training. She proved them wrong many times.

I am not a teacher of this art just a student, but I wish to share a bit of what I have learned on my journey as martial artist to learn. As part of my mother's family, Scottish Seafarers and my wife's comes from Hawaii, they were Filipinos who came there to work coffee plantations. They bought a coffee farm and raised children there. Their families intermarried with others. So yes, I have family members who are part Native Hawaiian. We have had much talk about martial arts, several of our family is law enforcement. I have been interested in the martial art throughout my life and have taught publicly for 20 years.

I have learned the Hula and Lua have many links but that does not surprise me. It is not just story telling. There is a training component to it. One of the points Kuma Michelle Manu used to make was about lazy dancers, she would say the animals, the kids, the parents and grandparents must be part of the dance. She would see look at how they are being lazy and only the kids and animals and working. She would tell us do not be lazy in your training!

Traditional Native People dance has been one of the methods of teaching movement to people. If you can dance you have sense of timing and distance. I say to be a good fighter you must have good timing, rhythm and fluidity.

Lua is different from other martial arts in that it revolves around breaking bones and dislocating joints. To do that Lua uses biting with the fingers to tear the skin and dig into the muscle, this was done for pain compliance to open the door for dislocation and joint breaking. There is also the pounding of Poi, these strikes are hard strikes done at joints. So as you can image the training is not easy. You do get battered and bruised in training. So if you wish to not get battered and bruised do not train in this art.

Lua also has healing components in it not just fighting. Like all old arts fighting and healing were together. If damage someone then you should be able to heal them as well.

Lua was not taught to everyone, and there were different levels of training. There was the basic level taught to the commoners and the advanced levels taught to the Chiefs and their elite warriors.

Even the idea of teacher non-native Hawaiian people was considered for forbidden for a long time. It has only been in my life time that it has been shared with non-natives. Lua taught in village schools and there were a number of different Lua schools at one time. But due to the missionaries coming in and changes in government the old ways were pushed away.

Today I only know of two surviving Lua schools. It was Solomon Kaihewalu's school who brought to non-Hawaiians. He faced many hard hurtles in doing so. It was not an easy path for him, as it had been forbidden to teach others it took some really amazing work to get the permissions from the elders.

Solomon Kaihewalu started teaching Lua to non-Hawaiians while stationed at a U.S. Air Force base in West Germany, but he didn't introduce it to the American public until 1963, when he was stationed at an Air Force base in Colorado. The first people to get access to the art's basic techniques were commissioned and non-commissioned officers. However, he had to be careful with respect to what he revealed because ancient customs forbid him from spreading the fighting methods off the island. What was called Ka'Pu'. That means forbidden.

He had creed that he believed in and lived it so I will share it with you the reader-

The Mana of the Kaihewalu 'Ohana Lua

It is the responsibility of the head of our 'Ohana Lua to observe, remember and bring the positive things into the 'Ohana Lua and omit those that are not.

The eyes of our 'Ohana Lua are used to watch where we step in life so as not to upset others. We make sure we see where we are walking, rather than stepping forward or backwards blindly, so we do not trip or fall on those we do not see.

The hands of our 'Ohana Lua are the children we embrace so they too can reach out and embrace and help others. They keep those from entering our home who want to cause problems.

The bodies of our 'Ohana Lua must stay strong and healthy. The body is like a tree trunk with branches, stems and leaves representing how we walk, jump, run, and kick, but they must be nurtured and taken care of or they will die and be of no use. The brain and heart act as the center of the body to help store the knowledge and wisdom of our 'Ohana Lua.

Considered as a whole, they form the body that keeps the family strong and together, and can reach out to others to help them by serving and sharing the food of our 'Ohana Lua.

Battle Tactics

What were some of the tactics used? Hawai'ian combat units of old consisted of groups of small squads, units and divisions. The squads and units were broken down into groups of 10, 20, and 30 warriors. A full division consisted of a total of 40 Koa. Each squad of 10 men were experts in several types of weapons they brought with them into combat.

As the Lua weapons (Mea - Kaua) descended like rainwater upon their enemies, the front of the Koa combat units started their advance to encircle their enemy. When the circle was completed the full division of 40 Koa closed the gap on the enemy. Now the Koa were ready to use the Ko'oko'o (bo - cane) and their smaller weapons, the Ka'ane (strangling cord), Lei-o-mano (shark tooth weapon), Pâhoa (single edge dagger), Maka Pâhoa (the eye, belly button, groin, double edge dagger), Newa (club), and Pâlua Pu'ili (double clubs) to finish off and conquer the enemy.

So to understand any ethnic martial arts you must understand about the culture and it's terminology. Here is more to learn:

Kapu-Forbidden

Peku-Kicks

Paa Lima-Hand Catch and Trap

Hikua-Throws

Ku'I Ku'I strikes/punches

Waho/Loo Hio- leg sweeps

Ihe Manamana Lima- spear finger poking

Pahu/Huki-Push & Pull methods

Nahu Waha- Biting with the mouth

Ku i- Punch, Poke

Mokomoko-everything goes fighting

Traditional Weapons

Hoe – Canoe paddle (oar),

Hoe Lei-o-mano – Oar, Shark tooth weapon,

Iwi, Ka'ane – Strangling cord

Ko'oko'o – Staffs (Long and Short)

Ku'eku'e Lei-o-mano – Knuckle duster weapon

Ku'eku'e Lima Lei-o-mano – Knuckle duster weapon,

Lei-o-manô – Shark tooth weapons

Maka Pâhoa – Double-edge (eye) dagger

Newa – Short (small) club,

Pahi – Knife,

Pâhoa – Single-edge dagger

Maka Pâhoa Ko'oko'o – Cane double-edge dagger, etc.

    Because warfare was a constant issue between the various rulers of royalty on islands, the use of everyday items were turned into weapons. Then there was true weaponry as well. Spears were used to hunt and well as fight. Warfare was very organized with ranks of fighters and their weapons. A typical battle used long range weapons first, this was the sling and the spear. Barrages were used in the fight to reduce the number of fighters. So slings and the ability to hit small targets were a strong skill. There are stories of the Hawaiians using slings to knock down fruit from trees was a show of skills. Both men and women were quite skilled with it. Women at times would keep slings tied around their necks like scarf so it was there when needed.

    One of the tactics was a flotilla of ships would pull on to a beach and the raiding party would organize and attack the village. Parties were organized into squads of 40 typically. Sometimes a fake raining party was sent out and the warriors would hide in the water and wait for the defenders to come and burn the ships. The warriors would use the paddles as weapons after hiding in the water.

Chapter 5 Introduction to Traditional Weapons

"Hoe" Canoe Oar

The oar was used as a tool to power and steer the outrigger canoes. The flat part of the paddle was used to protect and shield the Koas' (warriors') face and body, from objects thrown at the Koas. The flat edge side of the Hoe was used to chop down and cut their opponents. The handle was used to fight with as a staff or as a long Bo staff. The Hawaiian Oars were built, prepared and used 4 different ways during times of war.

Long Handled Oar (Hoe)

The long handled oar (Hoe) used as a paddle for outrigger canoes for paddling and steering. This is basic defense against an overhead strike with from a staff, a long stick or any two handed weapon being struck at the center of your head. Left Lead Left hand holding the paddle blade and your opponent is in Right lead.

Your grip is shoulder width apart with two hands, left thumb is up and right thumb is down in your grip. Weapon is held about nipple line and your feet are in a left lead. Blade of the paddle is on your left side. Your weight is even but not planted. Body position is strong to strike then you will move. You are blocking with the Hoe at mid shaft being center using it to strike your opponent's knuckles to break their grip on the weapon as they come in with an overhead strike. Using that strikes energy rotate to the left side and strike your opponent's head with the blade portion of the paddle. This is a stunning strike only. Then take the paddle edge and go over their head trapping it by locking it against your body with your left side. Pull them into you. The right hand is pushed up the shaft against their weapon locking it. This is done quickly, now throw them to the ground by using a cork screw motion by stepping backward with the left foot and setting forward with the right foot and twisting. The body goes where the head and neck goes. They are thrown head first to the ground mostly likely landing on their side to their back. Use the handle end of the shaft to clear their weapon if they retain it, then give a full strike like chop with the blade end of the paddle to the body. To keep them from moving away, use your knees to pin them.

    Right Lead with right hand holding the paddle blade and your opponent is in left lead. Your grip is shoulder width apart with two hands, right thumb is up and left thumb is down in your grip. Weapon is held about nipple line and your feet are in a left lead. Blade of the paddle is on your right side. Your weight is even but not planted. Body position is strong to strike then you will move. You are blocking with the Hoe at mid shaft being center using it to strike your opponent's knuckles to break their grip on the weapon as they come in with an overhead strike. Using that strikes energy rotate to your right side and strike your opponent's head with the blade portion of the paddle. This is a stunning strike only. Then take the paddle edge and go over their head trapping it by locking it against your body with your right side. Pull them into you. The left hand is pushed up the shaft against their weapon locking it. This is done quickly, now throw them to the ground by using a cork screw motion by stepping backward with the right foot and setting forward with the left foot and twisting. The body goes where the head and neck goes. They are thrown head first to the ground mostly likely landing on their side to their back. Use the handle end of the shaft to clear their weapon if they retain it, then give a full strike like chop with the blade end of the paddle to the body. To keep them from moving away, use your knees to pin them.

This method lends itself well to being used with a wooden boat oar, kayak paddle, musket, wooden stocked musket or long rifle, boat hook or similarly weighted tool or weapon. Adjustments are made if the angle is not directly overhead by the attacker. This method works down to about the chest level. It is easy to see how this would be done with weapons and items from the early 1800's.

Maka Pahoa/ Maka Pâhoa Ko'oko'o

The Maka Pahoa is pole weapon with a forked end, it held in both hands with the attacking end held in the left hand to go with the left lead being the attacking side. The weapon is held at shoulder height to guard against a center line strike to the head. The block is done with weapon held horizontally and striking the knuckles of the upper hand of the attacker swinging the weapon. The defense is then followed up with to the right side using the butt of the shaft. Push off with the back foot (right) and rotate the hips. There is a digging with the end of the shaft tracing down the arm. Then a vice lock done to the fingers of the opponent fingers with a pole to pole lock. With this there is a foot sweep to the lead foot while twisting at the hip. This is to throw them to the ground. Use the pointed end (forked) to stab them in the mid-section of the body. The body is pinned with the knees like in the previous method then followed up with strike using the butt of your weapon while standing back up with your knees slightly bent.

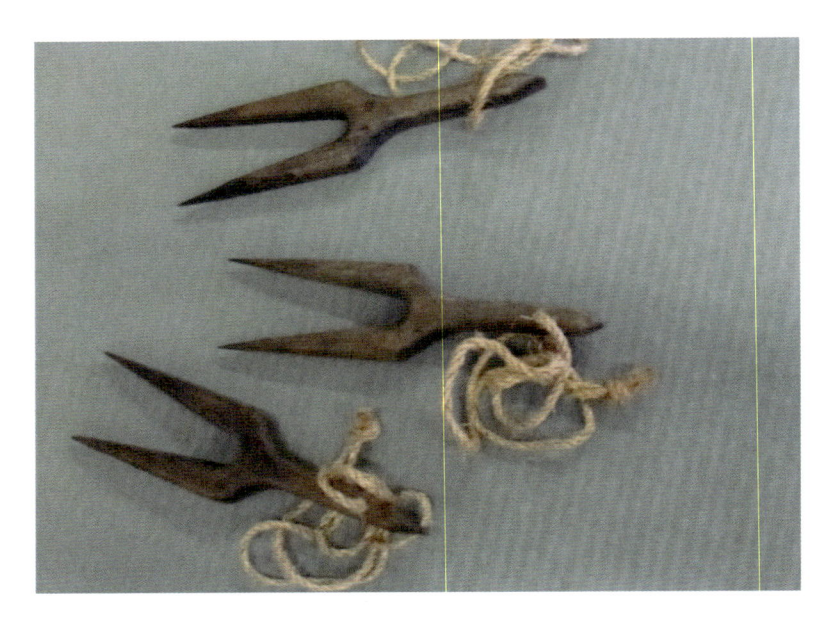

Maka Pâhoa - (Double-Edged Eye Dagger)

    The double (eye) pointed dagger can be used for offense and defense and can be used 3 different ways to defend one's self: clubbing, trapping of the hands, and poking.

    It is a forked weapon with a cord attached. It is held in the right hand, with cord attacked to the wrist with a larks foot loop. The left side is to be used with the left leg forward. The left hand is empty using an empty hand parry against a stab to the midsection by your opponent, this is followed up with a strike with the midsection (the U section) of the Maka Pahoa to your opponent's head. Then it is brought down to trap the limb, note is traces down the body. The limb is secured against body and a backward hip throw is used, pressure is used by the left hand to steer the body. Note the knees are bent feet are switched for the throw. The opponent's body is thrown to the ground, the body is pinned with the knees and stab is delivered to the face. A second stab is delivered by flipping the weapon around into the left hand.

Maka Pahoa Method #2

Defense against an outside method against a stab to the centerline on the midline. Step left and get off-line. Parry with left hand and strike with the Maka Pahoe using the right hand to parry the limb away. A trap is done with a scooping motion using the weapon. Step in with the right foot. The left hand goes to the neck/ collar, the right hand and the weapon goes to the front of the throat. Using a twisting motion throw them to the ground. Again the body is pinned with knees, switch hands with the weapon and deliver a stab to the body. The Left knee pins the Right arm away from the body.

Ku'eku'e Lei-O-Manô (Knuckle Duster Weapon

Knuckle Duster at US Army Museum Honolulu, Hawaii

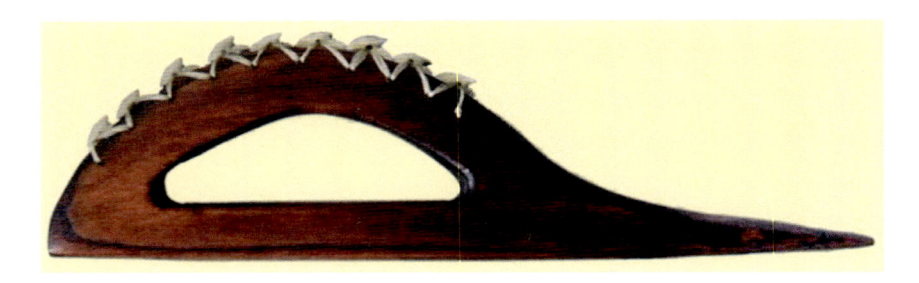

Ku-Efu-e Knuckle with Point

The Knuckle duster weapon is used for close range fighting. According historians some warriors carried this weapon to clean up the attackers when a wounded attacker went down. Typically it would be older warriors because of it's light weight.

Ku-Efu-e' is a knuckle duster weapon typically with a spike on the end of one side. It can be used in a defensive manner against a stab to mid-section of the body. You are in a right lead position, step in with your left foot while parrying with your left hand to the left outside to parry it. The hand is in a palm down with the fingers pointing up. The parry is down at the wrist of your opponent, the right hand is holding the Ku-Eku-'E delivering a ripping motion upward with the butt spiked end of the weapon in a diagonal angle. With pommel pointing upward and the point is down. Then come down to the parried limb raking the inside of the wrist while lifting and rolling the weapon hand of the opponent over. Shift your body weight right while raking your opponent's body with the jagged ends. Finish with a strike to the face then hook the neck with the pointed end turning them around while holding their wrist and pulling them backward, Once on the ground pin them with your knees and stab weapon to your opponent's rump to the Vegas nerve. This was done to cripple them and keep them from running away.

Knuckle Duster Method #2

Defense against a stab to your body by an attacking opponent. You are in a left lead stance with weapon in your right hand. Weapon is held at slightly above waist level. Step forward and to the outside quickly parrying with palm check parry to the attacking limb, make sure your fingers are pointing upward. Use a downward strike with butt of the weapon. They may or may not drop the weapon, target is mid-forearm for the strike. Then rail up side of the body as you are on the outside line. Apply a V- Lock to the neck and step back with your right foot for spinning throw to put them face down in the ground. Use your left knee to pin the body and punch to the face with the Right hand still holding your weapon using the D guard like Brass Knuckles.

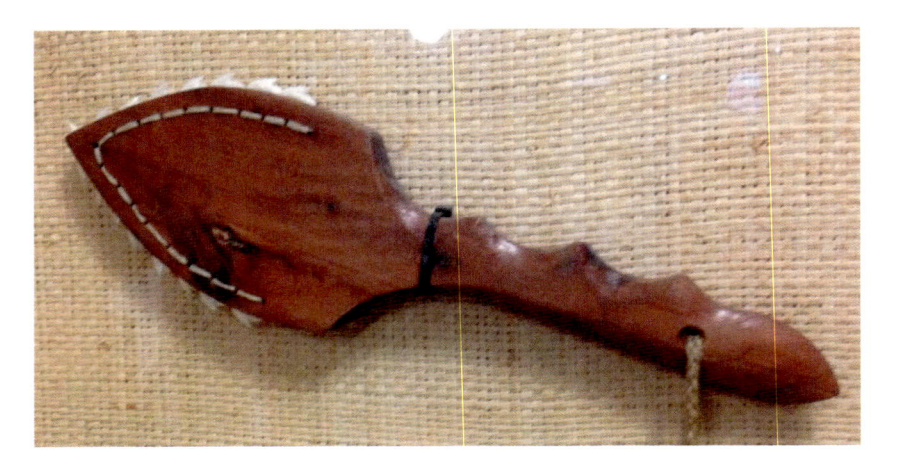

Lei-omano

Lei-omano has wrapped around shark's teeth. Some have described it like an elephant's ear. Other's say it looks like a Taro Leaf. It was modeled after the hand. It is used to strike with edge and the butt. The butt end is sharp so it can stab, hook and grab limbs. It too has a cord attached that handle that was used as weapon and for retention of the weapon in battle. The cord is attached to your limb using a lark's foot loop on the weapon hand.

    Defending against a thrust to the midsection using this weapon by an attacker. In the left lead position, step to the outside quickly while parring with your empty left hand, use a parry block with palm with your fingers pointing, fingers are together. Use the flat of the weapon to strike the right hand of your attacker, then slide your weapon up the arm to the body like rail. Shoot the arm around the neck to put them into a V-lock around the neck, step back with right foot and throw them to the ground face down. Stab with butt end, grab hair and pull heap up while cutting the throat.

Lei-o-mano Puka (Shark Tooth Weapon)

This weapon is designed to cut and spear your attacker. This is a light weight weapon and normally is carried by an older warrior or chief. Most elderly warriors carried this light weapon to clean up and take care of all those fallen opponents (warriors) who went down due to being wounded. The elderly warrior's job was to keep moving, taking the wounded to safety. The light weight of this weapon kept the elderly warrior from becoming overly fatigued.

Double Cord with Grab Stick- Ka' Ane

This Lua weapon is used in four different ways in combat. These are Blocking, Grabbing or Catching, Flipping and choking or Strangling

Ka'ane -Defense with Double Cord against a stab to the mid-section by a knife. This is the method against a person who is in a left lead holding their weapon in their right hand. Hold the tied cord in both hands like fist. Step to the outside with a left lead while striking with the bottom of your fist that is holding the wooden grab stick. The motion is like pounding the table. Strike the right wrist, use your left and pound the forearm with your left again like pounding the table. Poi pounding is what this method is called. Apply pressure with the cord, it is held taut while sliding up the arm. Use the arm as track for this motion. Then a right strike to the jaw while wrapping the neck. The pressure is applied with a V-lock to the neck, then a reverse throw is done while spinning them to the ground. They are thrown face down. Both knees are applied to the body while choking them. The cord is wrapped and twisted while tightening for choke.

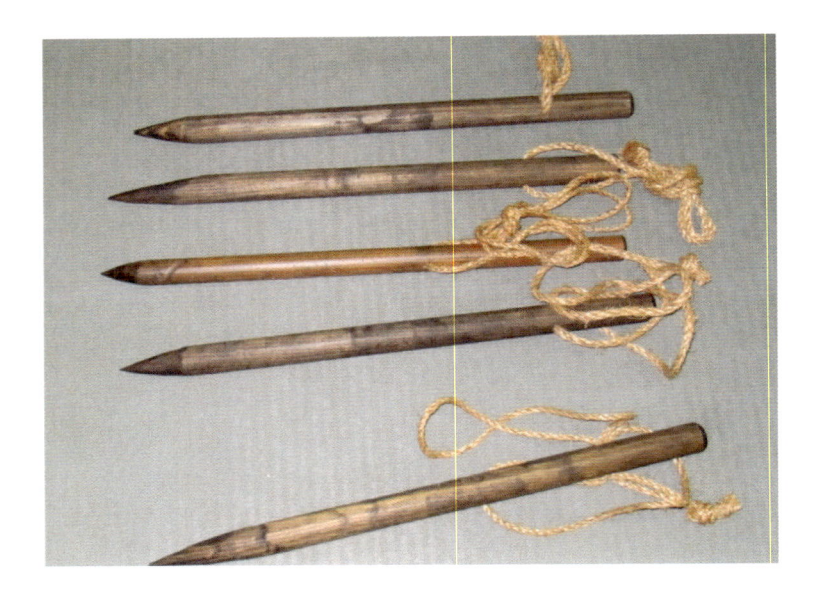

Pahoa

It is a sharpened stick used as single edged dagger for blocking, spearing, clubbing and strangling; it is attached to the right wrist via a doubled cord. It is used for striking, stabbing and swatting motion; the butt end is used for trapping a limb.

Defense against a right lead stab attack by a knife or sharp stick to your middle section, you are in a left lead, pivot with your right foot off line, palm check with left hand while striking with your weapon to their right wrist. Then stab across the ribs with your weapon in slicing motion, step behind them while slipping your cord around the neck with the stick pointed down, your right arm is like the water pump with left arm hold the base, shift your weight to throw them to the ground so they land face down. Hold on to the cord, mount them and use the stick and cord to choke your attacker.

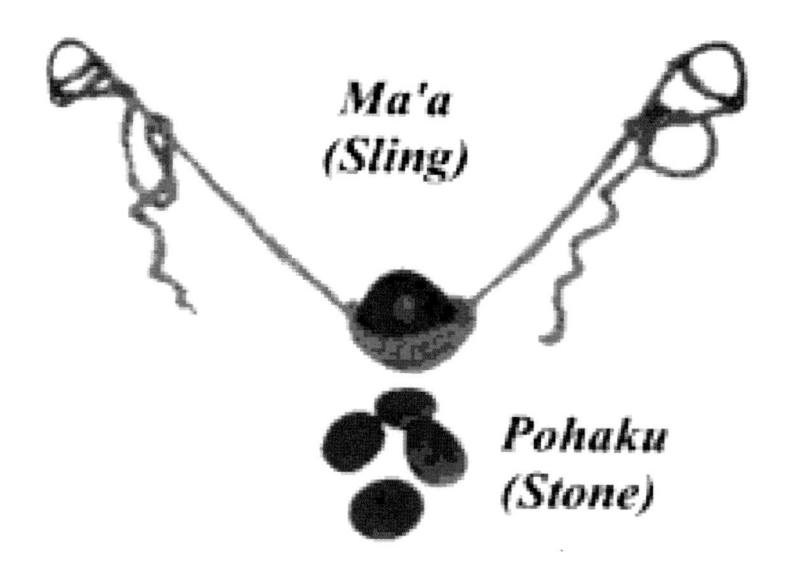

Ma'a
(Sling)

Pohaku
(Stone)

Here is one for throwing Dog Tennis Balls for sale on Etsy

     Some of these Lua weapons are the Ma'a (Sling) and the Pohaku (stone). The Ma'a is used to throw Pohaku high into the air to rain down on top of the enemy and is quickly followed with Polol û (long spears, from 6 feet to 18 feet long) also raining down upon the enemy.

Pohaka

Hoe Lei-o-mano (Oar - Shark Tooth Weapon)

The flat side of this weapon is used to block objects thrown at your face, as well as oncoming weapons. The entire length of this weapon is used as the Bo or Ko'oko'o (staff) in defensive fighting. The handle is designed to spear your attacker and the teeth of the shark are used for cutting.

Iwi, meaning Bone or bone from the Human. It once was considered and cherished coming from the dead. The Thigh Bone, the Shoulder Blade, the Hipbone, the Collarbone, the Forearm bone, the Rib Bone - these bones were once used as spears and knifes

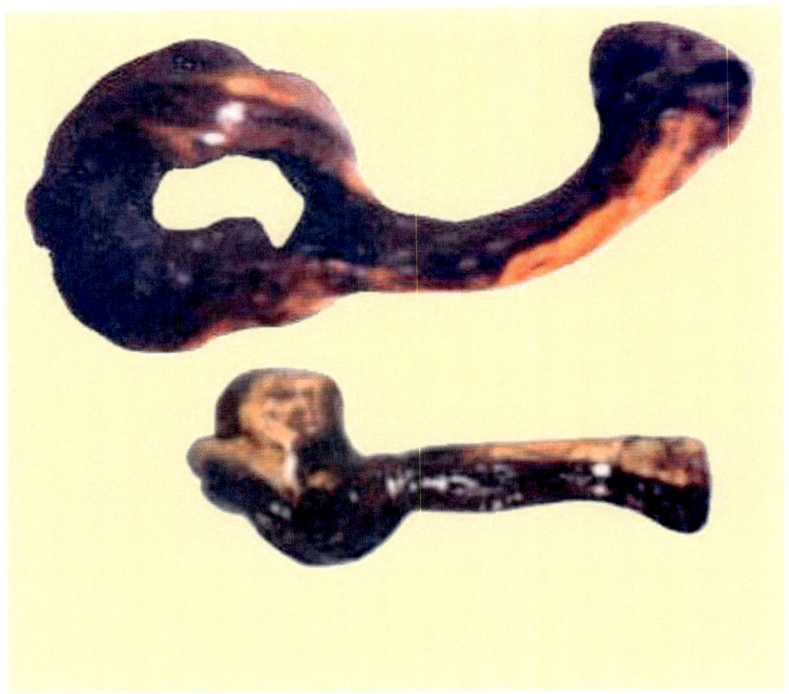

These clubs are from the roots of trees and were designed to look like the hip and leg bones of a human. This type of weapon is used to hammer, pound, cut and club a warrior's opponent.

The Weapons of Lua
Pahi (Knife)

The old Hawaiian wood Pahi (knife) is designed to do as much damage as possible. Most old Hawaiian wood knives are made to spear, poke, cut, and club with a single motion all at the same time.

Chapter 6
Hand-to-Hand Combat

When a warrior lost his weapon, he began hand-to-hand combat, or free-for-all against the enemy. This is called Ku'i Ku'i (boxing) and followed up with Mokomoko (dirty fighting, free for all, or go for broke).

Ka-piko-o-Wakea-The Navel of Wakea

Defender stands in the neutral position hands to the sides with hands closed like fists.

The attacker is in a left lead striking with a fist swung like a club to the left side of the defender's head.

The defender steps back with his right foot while blocking the strike with his left forearm with an outward block.

The defender quickly counter thrust with his right hand shaped like spear palm down into area just above the navel, knocking the wind out of the attacker.

Nahu-a I ke-kileo-i-pa'a-Bite to Neck at the Larynx

The defender has deflected the punches or the grabs by the attacker, then quickly grabs hold of the attackers shoulders with both hands.

Closes to hold attacker's shoulder with both hands, locking his hands (one hand grabs the other wrist) behind the attacker's neck.

The defender violently jerks the attacker towards him so that he can bite the esophagus (Adam's apple area) of attacker to suffocate the attacker. This method was done kill someone trying to kill the defender.

Ka-pa'ia-kuli The Defending Blow

Defender is in the neutral stance hands to his side fists closed.

The attacker rushes to place a choke on the defender's neck.

The attacker uses a two handed choke.

The defender breaks his attacker's choke hold grip by putting his hands together in the prayer position shooting upward using his forearms.

The defender then rotates his wrist outward striking and spreading his attacker's arms outward.

The defender quickly then counter attacks by striking his opponent's ears with open palms trying to damage his attacker's ear drums.

Ka-ihu-manumanu-the Blunted Nose

The defender is in a neutral stance with hands to his side fists closed. The attacker is in a left lead position and throws a punch from his right from the belt level. The defender side steps left while at the same time striking his attacker's downward with a forearm block and palm check in turning motion. The defender pivots back while countering striking with an uppercut thrown from the hip to the nose/upper lip of his attacker while checking the attacker's arm to the defender's body at the waistline.

Ka-ihu-akala Pink Nose Method-1

Defender is in a neutral stance with arms by his sides and his hands closed. The attacker is in a left lead with arms up ready to punch with a right to the body. The defender shifts and turns while side stepping with his left because the defender punches at his right midsection. The defender also block strikes the attacker's right forearm with his left hand and forearm. The defender then counter attacks with strike to the attacker's nose with the right edge of his palm. His palm is facing upward for the strike. The target can be the nose, upper lip or lower lip area.

Chapter 7 Practice Drills with Weapons

All martial arts you need drills that you can practice to remember what your teacher taught you. You must have way of practicing when you have no one else to train with. Otherwise that martial art will die off like a dinosaur. This is done in other arts as forms. Some arts teach it as dance, others as Shadow-fighting. All that being said I am including forms that I developed based upon what is described above as methods of fighting.

Drill #1

You must visualize this attack as described! Practice by yourself, if needed make simple training dummy to work with.

This is basic defense against an overhead strike with from a staff, oar, musket, stick or any two handed weapon being struck at the center of your head.

Start with Your grip is shoulder width apart with two hands, left thumb is up and right thumb is down in your grip.

Weapon is held about nipple line and your feet are in a left lead.

Blade of the paddle is on your left side, the blade is flat.

Your weight is even but not planted. Body position is strong to strike then you will move. You are in a left lead position.

You are blocking with the mid shaft being center using it to strike your opponent's top knuckles. Used like a punch block. You are stopping a strike to the middle of your head.

Using that strike's energy rotate to the left side and strike your opponent's head with the blade portion of the paddle.

This is a stunning strike only.

Then take the paddle edge and go over their head trapping it by locking it against your body with your left side. Your feet twist on the balls of your feet. Knees are slightly bent.

Pull them into you with your weapon

The right hand is pushed up the shaft against their weapon locking it.

This is done quickly, now throw them to the ground by using a cork screw motion by stepping backward with the left foot and setting forward with the right foot and twisting. (The body goes where the head and neck goes).

They are thrown head first to the ground mostly likely landing on their side to their back.

Use the handle end of the shaft to clear their weapon if they retain it,

Give a full strike like chop with the blade end of the paddle to the body.

To keep them from moving away, use your knees by dropping down on them to pin them to the ground. Knees should be below the shoulders and at the hips.

Drill #2

You must visualize this attack as described! Practice by yourself

This is basic defense against an overhead strike with from a staff, oar, musket, stick or any two handed weapon being struck at the center of your head and you are in a right lead instead of left lead.

Start with Your grip is shoulder width apart with two hands, right thumb is up and left thumb is down in your grip.

Weapon is held about nipple line and your feet are in a left lead.

Blade of the paddle is on your right side, the blade is flat.

Your weight is even but not planted. Body position is strong to strike then you will move. You are in a right lead position.

You are blocking with the mid shaft being center using it to strike your opponent's top knuckles. Used like a punch block. You are stopping a strike to the middle of your head in mid-swing.

Using that strike's energy rotate to the right side and strike your opponent's head with the blade portion of the paddle.

This is a stunning strike only.

Then take the paddle edge and go over their head trapping it by locking it against your body with your right side. Your feet twist on the balls of your feet. Knees are slightly bent.

Pull them into you with your weapon

The left hand is pushed up the shaft against their weapon locking it.

This is done quickly, now throw them to the ground by using a cork screw motion by stepping backward with the right foot and setting forward with the left foot and twisting. (The body goes where the head and neck goes).

They are thrown head first to the ground mostly likely landing on their side to their back.

Use the handle end of the shaft to clear their weapon if they retain it,

Give a full strike like chop with the blade end of the paddle to the body.

To keep them from moving away, use your knees by dropping down on them to pin them to the ground. Knees should be below the shoulders and at the hips.

Drill#3

The Maka Pahoa

The Maka Pahoa is pole weapon with a forked end the training one will be blunted!

This is for an attacker in right lead. It held in both hands with the attacking end held in the left hand to go with the left foot lead being the attacking side. The weapon is held at shoulder height to guard against a center line strike to the head.

The block is done with weapon held horizontally and striking the knuckles of the upper hand of the attacker swinging the weapon.

The defense is then followed up with to your opponet's right side using the butt of the shaft. Push off with the back foot (right) and rotate the hips.

There is a digging with the end of the shaft tracing down the arm. This is to loosen their grip on the weapon.

Then a vice lock done to the fingers of the opponent fingers with a pole to pole lock.

With this there is a foot sweep to the lead foot while twisting at the hip. This is to throw them to the ground.

Use the pointed end (forked) to stab them in the midsection of the body.

The body is pinned with the knees like in the previous method then followed up with strike using the butt of your weapon while standing back up with your knees slightly bent.

Drill#4 Maka Pahoa

It is held in the right hand, with cord attacked to the left wrist with a larks foot loop.

The left side is to be used with the left leg forward.

The left hand is empty using an empty hand parry against a stab to the midsection by your opponent,

It is followed up with a strike with the midsection (the U section) of the Maka Pahoa to your opponent's head.

Then it is brought down to trap the limb, note is traces down the body. The limb is secured against body and a backward hip throw is used, pressure is used by the left hand to steer the body.

Note the knees are bent feet are switched for the throw.

The opponent's body is thrown to the ground, the body is pinned with the knees and stab is delivered to the face.

A second stab is delivered by flipping the weapon around into the left hand.

Drill#5 Maka Pahoa

Defense against an outside method against a stab to the centerline on the midline.

Step left and get off-line.

Parry with left hand and strike with the Maka Pahoe using the right hand to parry the limb away.

A trap is done with a scooping motion using the weapon.

Step in with the right foot.

The left hand goes to the neck/ collar, the right hand and the weapon goes to the front of the throat.

Using a twisting motion throw them to the ground.

Again the body is pinned with knees, switch hands with the weapon and deliver a stab to the body.

The Left knee pins the Right arm away from the body.

Drill#6 Ku-Efu-e' Knuckle Duster

You are in a right lead position, step in with your left foot while parrying with your left hand to the left outside to parry it centerline thrust.

The hand is in a palm down with the fingers pointing up.

The parry is down at the wrist of your opponent, the right hand is holding the Ku-Eku-'E delivering a ripping motion upward with the butt spiked end of the weapon in a diagonal angle.

With pommel pointing upward and the point is down.

Then come down to the parried limb raking the inside of the wrist while lifting and rolling the weapon hand of the opponent over.

Shift your body weight right while raking your opponent's body with the jagged ends.

Finish with a strike to the face then hook the neck with the pointed end turning them around while holding their wrist and pulling them backward,

Once on the ground pin them with your knees and stab weapon to your opponent's rump to the Vegas nerve. This was done to cripple them and keep them from running away.

Drill#7 Knuckle Duster Method #2

Defense against a stab to your body by an attacking opponent.

You are in a left lead stance with weapon in your right hand.

Weapon is held at slightly above waist level.

Step forward and to the outside quickly parrying with palm check parry to the attacking limb, make sure your fingers are pointing upward.

Use a downward strike with butt of the weapon.

They may or may not drop the weapon, target is mid-forearm for the strike.

Then rail up side of the body as you are on the outside line.

Apply a V- Lock to the neck and step back with your right foot for spinning throw to put them face down in the ground.

Use your left knee to pin the body and punch to the face with the Right hand still holding your weapon using the D guard like Brass Knuckles.

Drill #8 Lei-omano

Defending against a thrust to the midsection using this weapon by an attacker.

In the left lead position, step to the outside quickly while parring with your empty left hand, use a parry block with palm with your fingers pointing, fingers are together.

Use the flat of the weapon to strike the right hand of your attacker, then slide your weapon up the arm to the body like rail.

Shoot the arm around the neck to put them into a V-lock around the neck, step back with right foot and throw them to the ground face down.

Stab with butt end, grab hair and pull heap up while cutting the throat.

Drill #9 Ka'ane -Defense with Double Cord against a stab to the mid-section by a knife.

This is the method against a person who is in a left lead holding their weapon in their right hand. Hold the tied cord in both hands like fist.

Step to the outside with a left lead while striking with the bottom of your fist that is holding the wooden grab stick.

The motion is like pounding the table very hard.

Strike the right wrist, use your left and pound the forearm with your left again like pounding the table. Poi pounding is what this method is called.

Apply pressure with the cord, it is held taut while sliding up the arm.

Use the arm as track for this motion.

Then a right strike to the jaw while wrapping the neck.

The pressure is applied with a V-lock to the neck,

then a reverse throw is done while spinning them to the ground.

They are thrown face down on the ground.

Both knees are applied to the body while choking them.

The cord is wrapped and twisted while tightening for choke.

Drill#10 Pahoa

Defense against a right lead stab attack by a knife or sharp stick to your middle section,

you are in a left lead, pivot with your right foot off line,

palm check with left hand

while striking with your weapon to their right wrist.

Then stab across the ribs with your weapon in slicing motion,

Step behind them while slipping your cord around the neck with the stick pointed down,

your right arm is like the water pump with left arm holding the base

Shift your weight to throw them to the ground so they land face down.

Hold on to the cord, mount them and use the stick and cord to choke your attacker.

Chapter 8 Making Your Own Training Aids

One of the great problems with any martial art is having training weapons that are safer than the real ones to train with. Lua has huge problem here as there is only one supplier for this on the West Coast. Most that are made are made as art pieces. That being said I will explain how I made my training aids.

One of the great challenges is copying weapons now only made for display. The size and weight should be as close to the originals as possible. I use hard wood scrap that I have in my workshop to make mine. Then later out of Mahogany and other nice hardwoods. Typically I use 1 inch hardwood. I cut out from a pattern my shape with electric jig saw. I used a 4-1 wood rasp for shaping. I sand with it with a homemade sanding block with 60 grit, then 80 grit then last but not least 100 grit sand paper. I stained mine and finished with varnish. I drill the shafts about 2 inches up and use 3/8 manila rope for my cord.

I have taken the liberty to take pictures of my trainers on large graph paper. The paper is 1 inch square graph paper. You can make a copy of the picture enlarge it up to 1X1 inch size then lay it on your wood to cut out the shape. Or if you wish lay out a 1 x1 grid on a piece of paper and scale up from the picture. Use the grid square by grid square method to transfer the size over. Simply put you copy with pencil in each square line by line.

I would say that you should open up the Y on the forked weapons to be big enough to catch a man's wrist. Mine were a bit on the small size when I first made them. Remember to blunt all points, practice slowly and carefully. Wear safety glasses for eye protection.

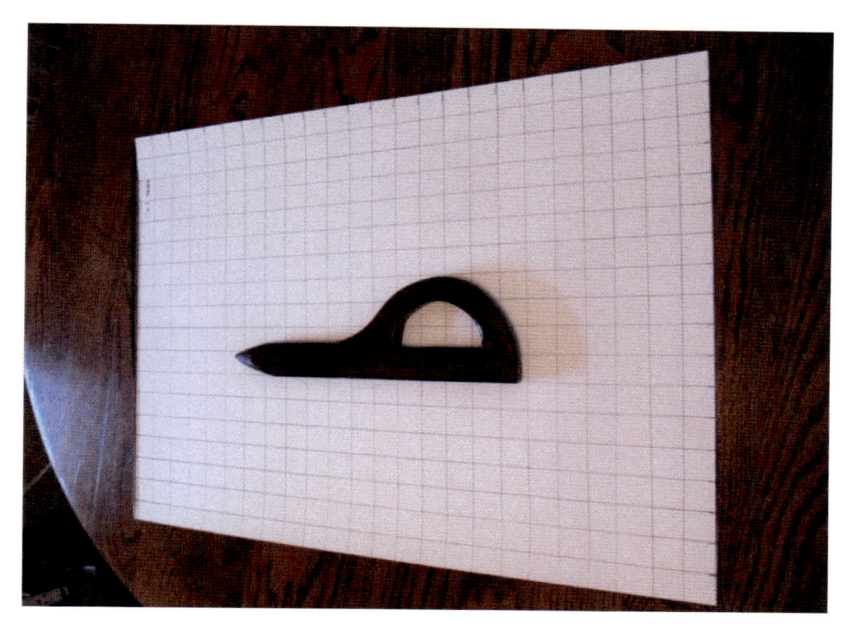

Ku-Efu-e' Knuckle Duster Trainer

Lei-omano Trainer

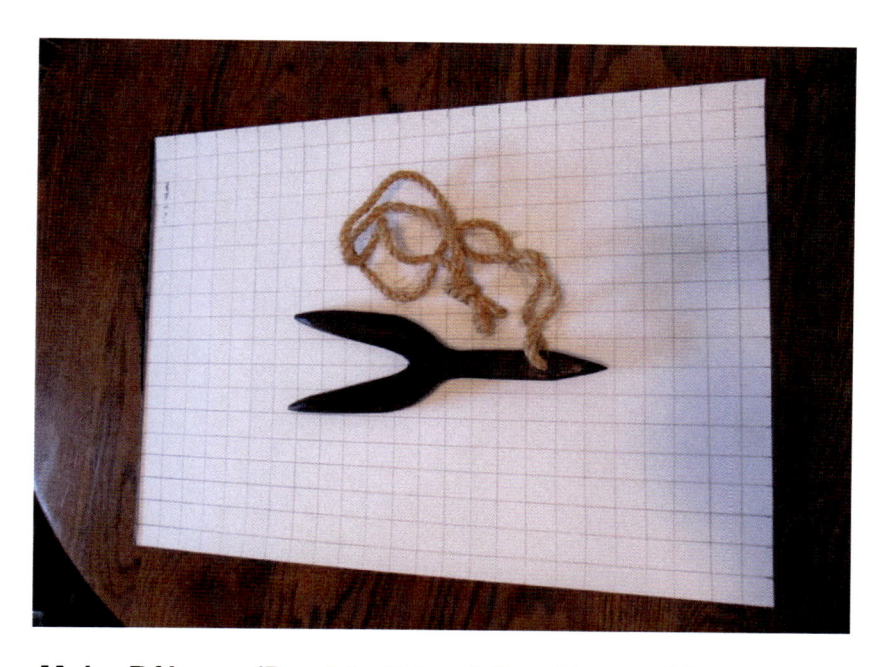

Maka Pâhoa - (Double-Edged Eye Dagger) Trainer with cord

Pahoa Trainer made from Rattan

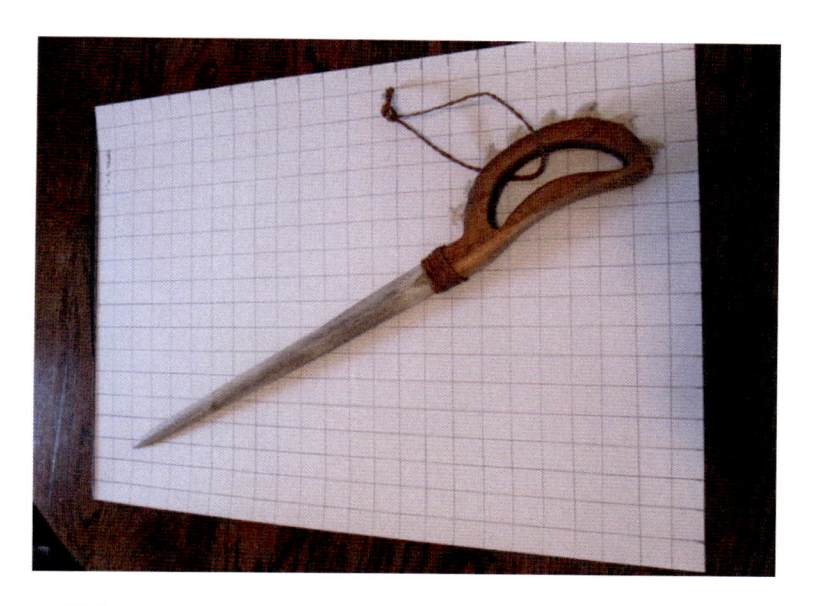

This is from my weapons collection. It is swordfish saber with a knuckle duster guard handle. It where Lua and Western Martial Arts came together.

Lei-omano not a trainer! Note the Shark teeth!

Chapter 9

In my time in the islands traveling and seeing family I have collected a number of pictures of many weapons I have seen there. Here I will share with you the reader a few of them.

Picture Collection from author's travels

Hawaiian Monarch Statue at Old Macadamia Nut farm
Big Island-Hawaii

New-made weapons collection for sale in Hawaii

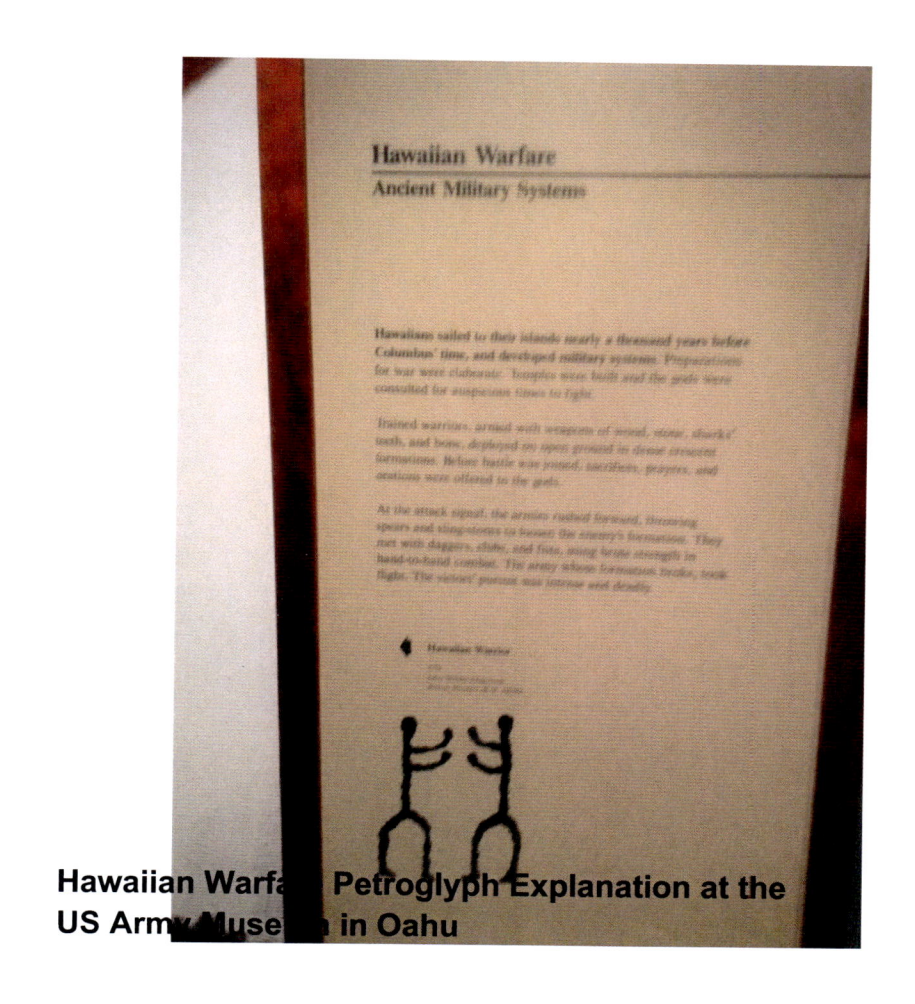

Hawaiian Warfare Petroglyph Explanation at the US Army Museum in Oahu

Hawaiian Royal Guard in the 1890s

Weapons display at US Army Museum Oahu

Weapons display at US Army Museum Oahu

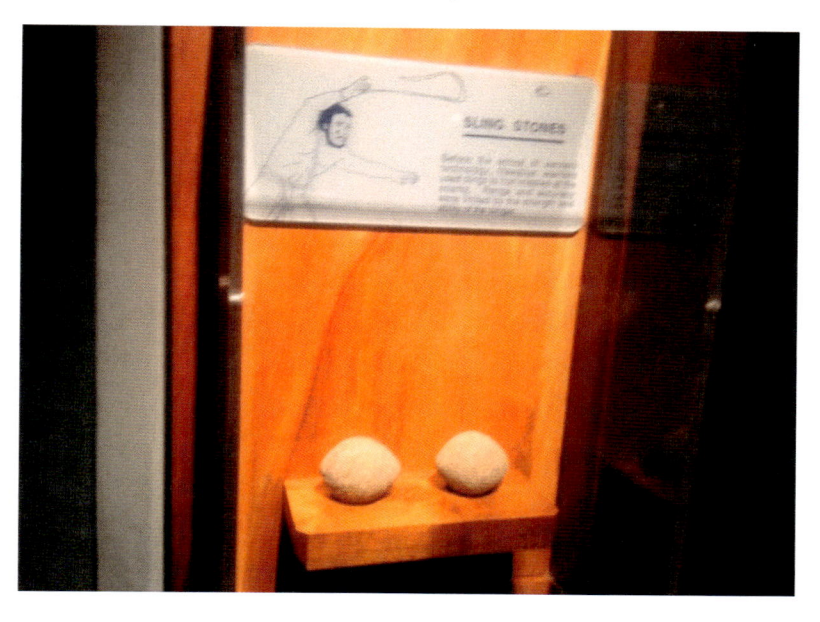

Sling Stones

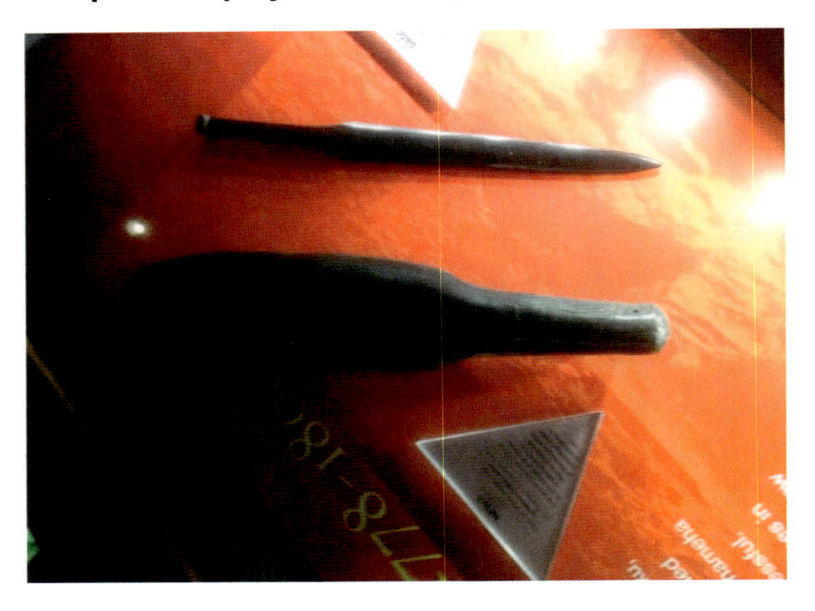

Weapons display at US Army Museum Oahu

Weapons display at US Army Museum Oahu

Hawaiian Outrigger model display at US Army Museum in Ohau.

Trainers for sale from iisports.com

83

Trainers for sale from iisports.com

Trainers for sale from iisports.com

Trainers for sale from iisports.com

Trainers for sale from iisports.com

References

Lua Art of the Hawaiian Warrior by Richard Kekumuikawaiokeola Paglinawan, Mitchell Eli, Moses Elwood Kalauokalani, Jerry Walker and with Kristina Pilaho' ohau'oli Kikuchi-Palenapa.

Ancient Hawaiian Martial Art of Kaihewalu "Ohana Lua"

https://www.learnz.org.nz/location192/bg-standard-f/polynesian-navigation

https://www.history.com/this-day-in-history/captain-cook-killed-in-hawaii

https://www.nationalarchives.gov.uk/education/resources/captain-cook-in-hawaii/

https://www.historynet.com/kamehamehas-commandos.htm

https://www.fortelizabeth.org/about-fort-elizabeth/

https://blackbeltmag.com/lua-the-ancient-hawaiian-martial-art-of-breaking-and-dislocating

https://blackbeltwiki.com/lua

http://coffeetimes.com/lua.htm

https://www.tourmaui.com/kamehameha-the-great/

http://www.hawaiihistory.org/index.cfm%3FPageID%3D273

https://www.gohawaii.com/hawaiian-culture/history

Made in the USA
Coppell, TX
12 March 2024